Stockton - B[...]
LIBRA[...]
Technical C[...]

Stockton & Billingham College

T018298

4339501003098442772601 2

KU-220-177

24[...]

26. [...]
10. MAY
10. MAR.
19. MA[...]
29. APR.
29. APR.

26. MAY

BY THE SAME AUTHOR

*Novels*

The Comforters
Robinson
Memento Mori
The Ballad of Peckham Rye
The Bachelors
The Prime of Miss Jean Brodie
The Girls of Slender Means
The Mandelbaum Gate

*Play*

Doctors of Philosophy

*Criticism and biography*

The Brontë Letters
John Masefield
Child of Light

*Poetry*

Collected Poems I

*Stories*

Voices at Play: stories and ear-pieces
The Go-Away Bird
Collected Stories I

# Collected Poems I

# MURIEL SPARK

# Collected Poems I

LONDON

MACMILLAN

MELBOURNE · TORONTO

1967

Copyright Muriel Spark 1952 © 1963, 1964, 1965, 1966, 1967

*Published by*
MACMILLAN & CO LTD
*Little Essex Street London* W C 2
*and also at Bombay Calcutta and Madras*
*Macmillan South Africa (Publishers) Pty Ltd Johannesburg*
*The Macmillan Company of Australia Pty Ltd Melbourne*
*The Macmillan Company of Canada Ltd Toronto*

Acknowledgments are made to the *New Yorker*, where
some of these poems were first published.

14839

821 SPA

*Printed in Great Britain by*
ROBERT MACLEHOSE AND CO. LTD
*The University Press, Glasgow*

Stockton - Billingham
LIBRARY
Technical College

FOR

EUGENE WALTER

# Contents

# Elementary

Night, the wet, the onyx-faced
Over the street was shining where
I saw an object all displaced
In black water and black air.

Was it myself? If so I found
An odd capacity for vision.
Capacity, I understand
Is limited by fixed precision,

Being the measure of displacement:
The void exists as bulk defined it,
The cat subsiding down a basement
Leaves a catlessness behind it.

That vision then, shall I concede is
Proved by a void capacity?
What's good enough for Archimedes
Ought to be good enough for me.

But knowing little of natural law
I can't describe what happens after
You weigh a body such as I saw,
First in air and then in water.

# Against the Transcendentalists

There are more visionaries
Than poets and less
Poets than missionaries.
Poets are a meagre species.

There is more vanity, more charity,
There is more of everything than poetry
Which, for personal purposes,
I wish may preserve
Identity from any other commodity
Also from Delphic insanity,
Drunkenness and discrepancy
Of which there's already a great plenty.
And so I reserve
The right not to try to
Fulfil the wilderness or fly to
Empyreal vacuity with an eye to
Publication, for what am I to
Byzantium or Byzantium
To me? I live in Kensington
And walk about, and work in Kensington
And do not foresee departing from Kensington.
So if there's no law in Kensington
Adaptable to verse without contravening
The letter to prove
The law, I'll make one.

The first text is
The word. The next is
(Since morals prevent quarrels

And writers make poor fighters)
Love your nieghbour, meaning
Your neighbour, let him love
His neighbour, and he his.
Who is Everyman, what is he
That he should stand in lieu of
A poem? What is Truth true of?
And what good's a God's-eye-view of
Anyone to anyone
But God? In the Abstraction
Many angels make sweet moan
But never write a stanza down.
Poets are few and they are better
Equipped to love and animate the letter.

I therefore resign
The seven-league line
In footwear of super-cosmic design
To the global hops
Of wizards and wops;
Hoping that if Byzantium
Should appear in Kensington
The city will fit the size
Of the perimeter of my eyes
And of the span of my hand:
Hands and eyes that understand
This law of which the third
Text is the thing defined,
The flesh made word.

# The Ballad of the Fanfarlo

Samuel Cramer, qui signa autrefois du nom de Manuela de Monteverde
quelques folies romantiques, – dans le bon temps du Romantisme, – est
le produit contradictoire d'un blême Allemand et d'une brune Chilienne.
BAUDELAIRE

I

Samuel Cramer came down in the lift,
Walked into the street and shut the door.
Behind him lay a settlement of fever,
The tremorous metropolis, before.

The first crossing that Samuel Cramer came to
A green light showed up and spoke to him,
'I see you are a man with fever on you
In the middle year of your time.'

The second crossing that Samuel Cramer came to
He stood beneath the yellow rays:
'I fear you are a man alarmed with fever
In the middle year of your days.'

The third crossing that Samuel Cramer came to
He saw a red light there,
And the light said, 'Halt, you feverish traffic
And tell me what you are.

'Now tell, now tell, your title and kind,
And tell, you feverish fellow
That wander this metropolis
From the green light to the yellow.'

'Oh I am Samuel Cramer,' he said,
'Born of a German father
Who was as pale as my naked bone,
And a brown Chilean mother.'

'And where do you come from, Samuel Cramer,
From the yellow light to the red?'
'I come from the dancing Fanfarlo.
She lies on her fever bed.'

'And where are you going, Samuel Cramer,
In the middle year of your time?'
'I go to seek my true friend,
Manuela de Monteverde his name.

'I wander this metropolis
In the good year of my prime.
By all the lights that are in the sun
I fevered go to claim
Manuela de Monteverde
Who is my heart's fame.

'The breath of my infection,
The water of my name,
Float in the null subtraction
That parted me from him,
Manuela de Monteverde
Who is my heart's fame.'

'Follow me, follow me, now Samuel Cramer,
My dear master to see
That sits in this metropolis,
For I think you lie to me.'

Samuel Cramer turned his footsteps.
The green light and the yellow said no word;
And he had come to a high hostel
With the red light for his guard.

Samuel Cramer went up in the lift,
Walked into a room and shut the door.
Behind him lay the streets of the tremorous city,
A steel desk and a chair, before.

'And what are you,' said the steel chair.
'With my little red light for a guard,
That come through the quivering streets of the city,
Where the green light and the yellow say no word?'

'My name is Samuel Cramer,' he said,
'Born of a Chilean mother
Who was as brown as my bone's marrow,
And a white German father.'

'Now if you are,' said the steel chair,
'Of a Chilean mother brown
And a white father from Germany,
Then you are No Man.

'And where do you come from, Samuel Cramer,
From the green light to the red?'
'I come from the dancing Fanfarlo
Laid out on her fever bed.'

'I think you lie, false Samuel Cramer,
Two times you lie,' the steel chair said,
'For a hundred years have come and gone
And the Fanfarlo lies dead.

'And where are you going, Samuel Cramer,
In the middle year of your days?'
'I seek Manuela de Monteverde
Who is my heart's praise.

'And all my nights of fever
And all my shifting days
Are an infernal river
Between my sight and his,
Manuela de Monteverde
Who is my heart's praise.'

'You lie, you lie, false Samuel Cramer,
Three times you lie as you stand there,
For Manuela de Monteverde
He is a steel chair.

'Now follow, now follow, Samuel Cramer,
Now follow my little red guard
To No-Man's sanatorium
In the antiseptic ward.

'And they shall rip you breast from back
And ask your white bone
If you are born of a German father
And a Chilean mother brown.

'They shall rip you lung and lights
And ask of your brown marrow
If you are come from the fever bed
Of the dancing Fanfarlo.

'And they shall rip you throat to thigh
And ask your false heart
If Manuela de Monteverde
Was ever of that a part.'


Samuel Cramer went down in the lift,
Walked through the tremorous streets with the little guard,
And he had come to No-Man's sanatorium
In the antiseptic ward.


'Now bless this day,' cried Samuel Cramer,
'That I have lived to win.
It is not for my white father
Nor for my mother brown,
It is not for the Fanfarlo
That the fever has put down,
But Manuela de Monteverde,
For his sake I'll suffer pain.'


Then up and said an ether-bowl,
'You bless this day too fine,
For in the antiseptic ward
I think you will feel no pain.'


'Then praise this day,' cried Samuel Cramer,
'That I have lived to see.
It is not for my Chilean mother
Nor for my father from Germany,
It is not for the Fanfarlo
That the fever has laid by,
But Manuela de Monteverde,
For his sake I'll die.'

Then up and spoke a little keen knife,
'You praise this day too high,
For in this sanatorium
I think you will not die.'

Samuel Cramer laid his head down,
And he was locked in an anaesthetic sleep.
The ether-bowl stood over him
And the keen knife ripped him up.

And first they found his white bone,
And next his brown marrow,
And when they found his feverish heart
They said, 'He is No Man that we know.

'If he is the son of a German father
And a Chilean mother brown,
Speak the word, you white bone.'
But answer they got none.

'If he is come from the Fanfarlo
That the fever has put down,
Speak the word, you brown marrow.'
But answer they got none.

'If Manuela de Monteverde
Was ever his benison,
Speak the word, you feverish heart.'
Answer they got none.

Then up and rose the little red light,
And he had run through the long streets of the city.
'Now hear, now hear, my master dear,
The news of my day's duty.

'Oh, they have asked his brown marrow
And they asked his white bone,
And they asked his false heart also,
But answer they got none.'

'He lied, he lied,' the steel chair said,
'Three times he lied as he stood here,
For a white father and a brown mother
Can never a man bear;
The dancing Fanfarlo is married
And buried a hundred years or more;
And Manuela de Monteverde
He is a steel chair.'

## II

The noise of a fog-horn out behind the window,
As well as the smell of gas,
And visible air of a metropolitan yellow,
And also the taste of withered cress,
And the chill feel of a zinc pillow:
All were assembled, having come concerning
Samuel Cramer, who woke before the morning.

'Whatever's in my nostrils is an element
No different from the mist I cannot see through,
And the same as a mouthful of sour condiment,
As it might be a cold white slab for my pillow.
In all I hear the siren vigilant:
Far away the fog must be on the river,
But where am I?' cried Samuel Cramer.

'The cloud, the taste, the smell, are feverish fancies;
The touch and the sound are past all reasoning;
For now I see a row of slender benches,
On each a narrow sleeper lying,
And every sleeper bound with bandages:
They must be in a hellish dormitory',
Cried Samuel Cramer, 'but where am I?'

'Oh, where am I, you slender sleepers?'
Then the four walls answered him,
'You lie in the convalescent ward
Of No-Man's sanatorium.'

A bell rang and the day came in
And every sleeper woke,
Peered through a slit in his bandages
As the four walls spoke.

Samuel Cramer looked at his own full length,
Saw that his long length was bandaged whole,
And he looked again at the narrow benches
And said, 'Who are you all?'

'Who are you all?' cried Samuel Cramer,
'And what were the ailments
That brought you to lie in this dormitory
All bound in hellish cerements?'

'I am No Man', said one, 'but I was a miller.
For several centuries I stood and ground
The daily grind, and was getting tired of it
Just when I met with my true friend,

Who being a miller of high ability
Turned the course of a whole river
To turn my mill, and still in my dreams I glorify
Manuela de Monteverde and enjoy him forever.'


'I was soldier,' said another; 'now I am No Man;
Served in all the big wars in every land
From Gaul to Brazil. Was working my ticket
Just when I met up with my true friend.
Now he was a soldier could take on an army
With catapult, cutlass or cartridge, and never
Came but he killed, and still I glorify
Manuela de Monteverde and enjoy him forever.'


'I was a scholar,' another said, 'early Dispontium
Was my special department, and I had come to the end,
As I had thought, of research on Dispontine manners
Just when I met my true and learned friend,
Who pointed out a significant point when he
In course of research was of course the first to discover
The Dispontii ate cross-legged, therefore I glorify
Manuela de Monteverde and enjoy him forever.'


'I was one,' said the next, 'who gathered impressions,
And now I am No Man, but there was a day
When I sat on the steps of cultural buildings
And watched the people passing by;
So bored, I almost would have done something about it,
But another sat beside me, and silent together
We communed with each other, and so I glorify
Manuela de Monteverde and enjoy him forever.'

'I knew the Industry inside-out
And now am No Man,' said another,
'But still I remember things were tight
Until I took up with a business partner.
He was a brilliant man, definitely.
Take his sales record. Look at the clever
Way he shoved those shares around. I glorify
Manuela de Monteverde and enjoy him forever.'

'Now one and all,' cried Samuel Cramer,
'In Manuela de Monteverde's name
I say he is a feverish poet
In the middle year of his time.'

Then each one cried, 'You false witness,'
And each sat up to testify
In Manuela de Monteverde's name,
And each one said, 'You lie.'

'You lie, you lie,' cried each to each,
And each to each arose,
And they had fallen all on all
And felled them with bitter blows.

They ripped them bandages from bone,
They ripped them bone and hair:
They were not done till everyone
Lay level in a smear.

The bones lay loose on the white zinc floor
In Manuela de Monteverde's name,
All in the convalescent ward
Of No-Man's sanatorium.

All in the convalescent ward
Of No–Man's sanatorium
A bell rang and the night came in
And settled over them.

'Now praise this night,' cried each to each,
'For I lie so bloodily
In Manuela de Monteverde's name,
And surely I shall die.'

Samuel Cramer lay on his loose bones,
Stared out of the window where there was
The new moon like a pair of surgical forceps
With the old moon in her jaws.

And in there came a bandage-roll
And a bottle of germicide,
And they had bound the loose bones
On the narrow benches laid.

The second day, a bell rang;
Then each to each called out,
'I fear that there's no dying here
But I shall rip your throat.'

And filament from ligament were parted
When in there came a roll of bandages
And a little bottle of disinfectant
To bind them up on the narrow benches.

And the third day they turned again,
And they had hacked them bone from bone.
'I see three ghosts,' cried Samuel Cramer then,
'They do not come too soon.'

'I see three ghosts,' cried Samuel Cramer,
'And they have come too slow.
The one is Manuela de Monteverde.
The next is the Fanfarlo.
The third is a fiend that hovers behind,
And he is no man that I know.'

Then in there came a bottle of germicide
With a roll of bandages,
All in the convalescent ward
To bind them up regardless.

### III

There was a sound of breathlessness by dawn;
Asthmatical, it changed into a yawn,
And Manuela de Monteverde bore
His bulky vapour up against the door.

Excogitated, it was tiresome
Being the fattest ghost in Christendom;
Looked at the narrow benches with regret,
Shuffled and lit a stubble cigarette.

And underneath an airy domino
Rattled the members of the Fanfarlo,
The ancient vertebrae inflexible
Still she contrived a clamorous *pas seul*;

Scattered her jewels in their sockets loose
That fell about her height in bright disuse.
All up and down the convalescent ward
Came she, a fabulous camelopard.

And there was another that hovered behind.
It was a fog that might have been a fiend
Or an angel caught in a cataleptic pause
For all it looked like anything that is.

And silent, with ambiguous intent,
This hovered in its own environment.
The air of No-Man's sanatorium
Seemed epileptic by comparison.

Samuel Cramer rose from his narrow bed.
'Now praise this day at last,' he cried.
'I see Manuela de Monteverde plain
Though he is fat that once was lean.

'I see you plain, my true friend
Who come so tardily.
In No-Man's sanatorium
For your sake I lie.

'And daily, daily, for your sake
I suffer my heart's bane
Which is destruction without death,
Destruction with no pain.

'And whether you were a false friend
Or whether you were a true,
Deliver me now from this limbo
    And I shall follow you.

'And I shall follow you night and day
In the world invisible,
And were you a false friend or a true,
I'll follow in Heaven or in Hell.'

Manuela de Monteverde spread
His open palms, sunk in the spongy wrists.
'Speaking as a ghost,' he said, 'I am a man
For whom the visible world exists.

'And if you should follow, my dear fellow,
No Heaven and no Hell would you see,
Nor love nor hate where I stagnate
In a limbo of sympathy.

'True, I was a false friend but first I was a true,
And I went to the grave, but never could forget
How all of you have magnified my name;
I have grown fat on that magnificat.

'And now am stuck in a deadlock of affection,
And I suppose, so long as I remember
The glory of man each man will glorify
Man and destroy him forever.

'So if you must follow, my dear fellow,
I think you should follow not me,
For I swear it's neither here nor there
In a limbo of sympathy.'

'Oh I must part from you,' said Samuel Cramer,
'And you must part from me,
But Manuela de Monteverde
My heart's fame will ever be.

'And I shall smite the light of the sun
And harrow the earth's face,
And I'll contend until I find
A way to depart in peace.'

All in the convalescent ward,
A bony ghost was rattling to and fro.
'I see my long, long, love,' cried Samuel Cramer,
'And she is the dancing Fanfarlo.

'I see you plain, my long, long, love,
And gawky is your tread,
And you have gone to skin and bone
Since you lay on the fever bed.

'Now whether you were a false love,
Or whether you were a true;
Take me away from my misery
And I shall follow you.

'And I shall follow you day and night
In the world invisible,
And were you a false love or a true
I'll dance with you in Heaven or Hell.'

'I can't stop now,' said the Fanfarlo,
'Although I'm short of breath,
For I'm employed on the skeleton staff
Of the dancing troupe of Death.'

She passed him by, and her step was high,
Over her shoulder calling shrill,
'After I lay on the fever bed
I rose and married well.

'I tired of that, and went to the grave,
But I could never forget
My macabaresque that was such a success
And my famous pirouette,

'Till Death, the talent-scout, took me up,
And now he hovers at my back
Like a fiend that looks like nothing on earth,
And I think that my bones will break.

'So if you would follow, my sweet fellow,
Be sure it's your vocation,
For there's no peace being caught like this
In a limbo of agitation.'

'Then you must part from me,' cried Samuel Cramer,
'And I must part from you,
But in Heaven or in Hell I shall remember
The dancing Fanfarlo.

'And I shall shift the files of the stars
Until the empyreal orders cease,
And I'll confound until I find
A way to depart in peace.'

All in the convalescent ward
A silent fog was hovering,
And it might have been leviathan
For all it looked like anything.

'Now Death I see you plain,' said Samuel Cramer,
'Oh you have come too slow.
Come out like a man and reason with me
For I would reason with you.

'For I am Samuel Cramer,' he said,
'And I am the natural meridian
Of a father and mother, north and south,
And am I not a man?

'Excellently I was virtuous
And viciously I sinned,
Slowly, slowly, lost my looks
Alas, and I'd read all the books
Before I came to No-Man's sanatorium
Where death is in my mind.'
Then Death spoke courteously to Samuel Cramer,
And Death said, 'Are you blind?'

'I am not blind,' said Samuel Cramer,
'And all things low and great,
That I have seen beneath the sun
I never shall forget.

'For I have seen the bright things and the black,
And I have seen enough
To make me as fit a man for Heaven
As I am for Hell, in my belief.'
Then Death spoke courteously to Samuel Cramer,
And Death said, 'Are you deaf?'

'I am not deaf,' said Samuel Cramer,
'And I have listened day and night,
And every word that I have heard
I never shall forget.

'For I have heard the innocent voice
And I have heard the foul,
And I am as fit a man for Heaven
As I am fit for Hell.'
Then Death spoke courteously to Samuel Cramer,
And Death said, 'Can you feel?'

'Oh I can feel!' cried Samuel Cramer,
For I have fondled cold and heat.
There's no transaction in all sensation
But I have had to do with it.


'For I have drunk the subtle water
And eaten the ruinous bane,
And I have smelt the melancholy vapour,
As well as the stanchless fume of carrion.
Each device of sin and grace
Has made me and undone.


'Now I am fit to be let beyond the sheer
Celestial pale, and driven
Before the glaciers that ride
All the precipitous streets of Heaven.


'And I am able to handle infernal cosmetics
And blacken my arms like vile
Branches that hoe the storm-sky,
Feverish culture of Hell.


'So I shall follow you night and day
In the world invisible,
And speak the fame of all I have done
To Heaven or to Hell.'


Then Death spoke courteously to Samuel Cramer,
And Death said, 'I admire your memory
And also the fame of all you have done,
Likewise your marvellous delivery.

'And for all you are gagged and riven here
You have my sympathy.
Now the fittest place for such a case
Is surely a limbo of memory.'

'But I'll not go to a limbo,' cried Samuel Cramer,
'And I have been gagged and riven
For nothing less than to go in peace
To Hell or to Heaven.'

Then Death said, 'Heaven is not my province
And Hell is not my territory,
So if you must follow, my true fellow,
I think you should follow not me.'

'But I shall follow you,' said Samuel Cramer,
'To the world invisible
Where I'll be free to hack my way
To the bounds of Heaven or Hell.

'Oh I shall rock the ethereal foundations,
Wherever the world invisible is,
And I shall rend until I find
A way to depart in peace.'

'The terms of departure in the peace treaty,'
Said Death,
'According to our annals,
Provide for a proper mortality
Only through the proper channels.

'And according to the formula
That I am furnished with,

There is a staple amnesia
That leeches to the pith.

'It's blind, it's blind, the keen-eyed kind,
It's deaf, the sedulous ear,
And words of legendary address
Swallow each other's pointedness
In the place where I transpire.

'This is the formula that moles
Its blind way to Heaven or Hell;
And sometimes in the last event
I hear a solitary call:
*Sever my ears in a hundred years
But let me listen a while.*

'And often I hear a lonely noise
Before the dark sets in:
*Make me null at a distant spell
But leave me rife till then.*
And mortified from every side
The voice of memory comes crying.

'It's *Hey, Death!* and it's *Hoa, Death!
Will you remember me?*
But there's no clause for a personal case
Laid down in the peace treaty.

'It's checked, it's checked, the retrospect,
It's lapsed, the sympathetic kind,
And agitation's under stress
Of a rigid absent-mindedness
In the place where I impend.

'So if you must follow, my true fellow,
I think you should follow not me,
For there's no scope for a talented type
In the loss of memory.'

All in the convalescent ward,
A bell rang, and the night came in,
And every man an enemy
On the narrow benches lying.

'I call you all,' cried Samuel Cramer,
'To witness my treachery
If I contract the false pact
That was offered me this day.

'And when the hawk shall creep in the earth
And hogs nest in the sun,
Then I'll forget the prime estate
Of all things I have known.

'When the lizard mates with Pegasus
And the lynx lies with the roe,
Then I'll forget the black and the bright
The high delight and the low,
Manuela de Monteverde
And the dancing Fanfarlo.'

# The Grave that Time Dug

This is the grave that time dug.
This is the box
   that lay in the grave that time dug.
This is the hand
   that rapped on the box
      that lay in the grave that time dug.
This is the stove
   that warmed the hand
      that rapped on the box
         that lay in the grave that time dug.

This is the child an instant born
   that lit the stove
      that warmed the hand
         that rapped on the box
            that lay in the grave that time dug.
This is the pink deceptive thorn
   that bled the child an instant born
      that lit the stove
         that warmed the hand
            that rapped on the box
               that lay in the grave that time dug.

This is the alderman bound and sworn
   that planted the pink deceptive thorn
      that bled the child an instant born
         that lit the stove
            that warmed the hand
               that rapped on the box
                  that lay in the grave that time dug.

# Elegy in a Kensington Churchyard

Lady who lies beneath this stone,
Pupil of Time pragmatical,
Though in a lifetime's cultivation
You did not blossom, summer shall.

The fierce activity of grass
Assaults a century's constraint.
Vigour survives the vigorous,
Meek as you were, or proud as paint,

And bares its fist for insurrection
Clenched in the bud; lady who lies
Those leaves will spend in disaffection
Your fond estate and purposes.

Death's a contagion: spring's a bright
Green fit; the blight will overcome
The plague that overcame the blight
That laid this lady low and dumb,

And laid a parish on its back
So soon amazed, so long enticed
Into an earthy almanack,
And musters now the spring attack;
Which render passive, latent Christ.

# The Yellow Book

They did not intend to distinguish between the essence
Of wit and wallpaper trellis. What they cared
Was how the appointments of the age appeared
Under the citron gaslight incandescence.

Virtue was vulgar, sin a floral passion
And death a hansom at the door, while they
Kept faith with a pomaded sense of history
In their fashion.

Behind the domino, those fringed and fanned
Exclusive girls, prinked with the peacock's eye
Noted, they believed, the trickle of a century
Like a thin umbrella in a black-gloved hand.

# Like Africa

He is like Africa in whose
White flame the brilliant acres lie,
And all his nature's latitude
Gives measure of the simile.

His light, his stars, his hemisphere
Blaze like a tropic, and immense
The moon and leopard stride his blood
And mark in him their opulence.

In him the muffled drums of forests
Inform like dreams, and manifold
Lynx, eagle, thorn, effect about him
Their very night and emerald.

And like a river his Zambesi
Gathers the swell of seasons' rains,
The islands rocking on his breast,
The orchid open in his loins.

He is like Africa and even
The dangerous chances of his mind
Resemble the precipice whereover
Perpetual waterfalls descend.

# *We Were Not Expecting*
# *the Prince To-Day*

As stated above, we were not expecting . . .
All the same, you had better show him the sleeping
Beauty upstairs with her powder still intact,
While the whole court on sentry duty, believe it,
Propped in their wigs a century exact,
Deplore her blunder, or rather, misconceive it.

And you had better and better deliver
The bat from her tresses, dispose for a kiss
That bluff on her webby mouth, for suppose he should call it,
And give her a nudge, and she take the hint, and this
Beauty be a cloud of powder over her pallet?

# Evelyn Cavallo

This person never came to pass,
Being the momentary name I gave
To a slight stir in a fictitious grave
Wherein I found no form and face, alas,
Of Evelyn Cavallo, Evelyn of grass.

Therefore, therefore, Evelyn,
Why do you assert your so non-evident history
While all your feminine motives make a mystery
Which, to resolve, arise your masculine?
Why will you not lie down

At the back of the neither here not there
Where lightly I left you, Evelyn of guile?
But no, you recur in the orgulous noonday style,
Or else in your trite, your debonair
Postprandial despair.

# A Tour of London

Anyone in this top-floor flat
This morning, might look out upon
An oblong canvas of Kensington
Almost ready for looking at.

Houses lean sideways to the light;
At foreground left, a crowd of trees
Is blue, is a footman, his gloves are white.
The sky's a pair of legs, top-right,
The colour of threadbare dungarees.

All the discrepant churches grind
Four, and in the window frame is
Picasso at least, his scene; its name is
*Morning*; authentic, but never signed.


II. KENSINGTON GARDENS

Old ladies and tulips, model boats,
Compact babies, mobile mothers,
Distant buses like parakeets,
Lonely men with mackintoshes
Over their arms – where do they go?
Where come from? now that summer's
Paraphernalia and splash is
Out, as if planted a year ago.

39

### III. WHAT THE STRANGER WONDERED

Where does she come from
Sipping coffee alone in London?

The shoes, the hair – I do not think
She has anything in the bank.

Has she a man, where is he then,
Why is she sitting at half-past ten

Reading a book alone in London?
Where does the money come from

That lets her be alone and sipping
Not with a man, not in a job, not with a dog
    to the grocer tripping?


### IV. DAY OF REST

The clock knocked off at quarter to three
And sat there yawning with arms stretched wide,
And it was set going again by nobody,
It being Sunday and we being occupied.

Therefore the day happened and disappeared,
But whether the time we kept was appropriate
To rend, to sew, to love, to hate,
No one could say for certain; all that occurred
Was Sunday, London, bells, talk, fate.

## V. SUBURB

It is the market clock that moonish glows.
Where two hands point, two poplars interlock.
Night's verities knock
Normal perspectives comatose,
Proving the moon a market clock,
The trees, time's laughing-stock.

## VI. THE HOUSE

Their last look round was happening when
The bus pulled up outside.
Nothing burning? Windows tried?
The lights go on and off again
And they are satisfied,
And we already starting off –
But see the house, how curious,
The lights again! and sure enough,
Feeling the catch behind the curtain
A hand – just to make certain.

## VI. MAN IN THE STREET

Last thing at night and only one
Man in the street,
And even he was gone complete
Into an absence as he stood
Beside the lamplight longitude.
He stood so long and still, it would
Take men in longer streets to find
What this was chewing in his mind.

# The Rout

A battle between thousands of bees and wasps in the ancient church at Stockerton, near Market Harborough (Leics.), has ended in a victory for the wasps.

Since the battle started three weeks ago the church has been closed and no services have been held.

For years, the bees had been storing their honey under the roof. But the honey started to trickle down the walls. The smell attracted the wasps.

Thousands of bees have been killed and the wasps are now eating the honey.

It is hoped to reopen the church on Sunday.

(NEWS CHRONICLE, 7 September 1951)

From Oliver Cromwell's despatch to Speaker Lenthall dated 14 June 1645, from Market Harborough:

'This day we marched towards him. He drew out to meet us. Both armies engaged. We, after three hours fight very doubtful at last routed his army; killed and took about 5,000; very many officers, but of what quality we yet know not. We took also about 200 carriages, all he had, and all his guns, being twelve in number; whereof two were demi-culverins and (I think) the rest sakers. . . . Sir, this is none other but the hand of God, and to him alone belongs the glory, wherein none are to share with him.'

## I

'has ended in a victory for the wasps'
What's wasps? –
A species of bees, or bees
A sort of wasps? Look
Them up in the Pocket Book of
British Insects: The Honey Bee,
Not a native of Britain.
After escape from captivity,
Wild colonies in hollow trees
Or similar sites not uncommon,
But these are from domesticated stock.

Wasps: A common wasp colony in
August or September may contain
Many thousands but all of these
Except the queens
Die in the autumn.


## II

'the honey started to trickle down the walls',
And that is sickening enough.
For years they stored the stuff under the roof
And summer had o'erbrimmed their clammy cells.
'And that is sickening enough', to use the phrase
Lawrence used about bees' ways;
('bees . . . cluster on their own queen.
And that is sickening enough.')
What Lawrence meant I mean,
Which is that humanity's
Different, or ought to be, from bees.
We who are of imported
Origin, wild or domesticated,
Are not so similar
To bees as wasps are,
But in smelling honey we
Are like enough to wasp and bee
To be what we ought not to be.


## III

'The smell attracted the wasps.'
Thousands of upstarts out of paper cells

Form up, assault the established
Wax-works of the wealthy sweet with smells
From long-ago ancestral summers ravished.

Wasps that recently have been
Clustering on your own queen,
Witness the outcome:
The murder of innumerable bees,
'A victory for the wasps' 'but these
Die in the autumn.'


### IV

To the Queen Wasp: a despatch from Buzzer Bummer
Dated nineteen–fifty–one, the end of summer,
From Stockerton church near Market Harborough:
    This day we marched towards her.
    She drew out to meet us. We,
    Since three weeks' fight at last routed her army.
    Took all stores. Killed many thousand.
    Madam, this is none other but the hand
Of God. 'The wasps are now eating the honey.'
'It is hoped to reopen the church on Sunday.'

# Four People in a Neglected Garden

Not yet. That is the high concession,
Taking the best of it.
Dying, not dead, the neglected garden
Is passionate yet.

But we are a process no protracted
Parley with trowel and gravel will prolong.
Nature nurtured us too, and then neglected
To gauge how long the grass grew long.

We four are gardens and are guardians
Of gardens. No wonder we let the increase
Of grass grow under our feet and made our own
Seditious separate peace.

Because there is a truce before the tall tree bending
Falls in the end and withers,
Ourselves the occasion of an afternoon's portending –
Lie, syringa; follow, rambler; stems, tumble together.

# On the Lack of Sleep

Lying on the roof of everything I listen
To the breath of ambition in her sleep, to the gasp of rancour
Turning in her dream. And the parting of lovers, the coming
    together
Of old divisions, the meeting and retreating of partners
        Cease, though I do not sleep.

Already I have wandered through fields of Michaelmas
    flowers. Tired
As I am, I remember the counting of all souls, think of their
    blue faces
I sought so long and discovered at last in the house
    below,
        Asleep, though I do not cease,

Though I persist into the day without motive as in the first
    hour
Of my life, tired as I am, I see the innocence I am left with.
Honour yawns, vanity foams in her coma, charity stretches
        A sham, luxurious limb.
Until I gather you again when I come into my own,
        Lie low, my sleepy fortunes.

# The Pearl-Miners

By night I watch a fitful tribe
Along the street advance and halt.
Time and again their limbs describe
A proud protracted somersault.

Blank-eyed beneath the lamp they steer
Compliant hips with hands of chalk.
I know them by their grief, and hear
Convulsions tolling in their talk.

They come, contemptuous and fleet
In tartan jeans, in ochre tights,
To make overt their counterfeit
Drowsy exotic appetites.

They are asleep and cannot rest,
Dismayed in far delirium.
Elaborately they attest
The dreaded labours still to come.

I know them by the lights of fear
On their elliptic faces falling.
This way and that, they haul the gear
And apparatus of their calling.

So obsolete, the block they drag,
So bitterly they drill and grind,
So deep beneath the pavement flag
They dig for pearls and do not find.

So freakish, they descend and storm
The black foundations, and in vain
They rise distracted to perform
Their supplicating rites again.

High-style they flash, akimbo fall,
Entreating on their shaken heads
That pale magnetic mineral
Which lugged them from their sundry beds.

Full-wheel the rounds revolve alike:
The sleepers turn, and cheek by cheek,
Dig up the road and do not strike
The lustrous milky seam they seek.

I recognise them by their fear;
So fair the dream, so far the sight.
The lambent virtues are not here
In Kensington of dreadful night.

Your boys of amber, quit your load;
You emerald, you marble girls,
Not underneath Old Brompton Road
Nestle the subterranean pearls.

I know these miners comfortless,
And by their pain identify
Pearl within pearl, since I possess
None but my bane to measure by,

None but their sleep to waken me,
None but their sorrow to confide
What pleasures have forsaken me,
None but my foe to be my guide.

48

I reckon only by their lack,
Rich within rich perfection furled,
And, by the sepulchre they hack,
Perceive the living underworld.

Here they have come, my fake, my lost,
My own familiars to their grave.
By vicious lights like elm-trees tossed,
Their bright pathetic branches wave.

So high the fault, the dream so true;
So low, the lovely mind persists
Immaculate, but not for you,
Dissevered, sad somnambulists.

# Omen

Here is the time of watching birds;
senses mingle and show their hands.
Now is the place where the signal stands

that points an omen from both my doors;
though the street shall talk like a hammer,
walls keep silence over my shoulder.

The wrong key in the right door
ponders the portent. Which window
saw where I have been to-morrow?

where I rocked my house on the water;
doors moved like an ark turning
back her face, and this is a meaning.

For the unlucky eye never shall taste
the bright bow of my vision again,
but this error, bitter as brine,

shall blind the eyes that heard the day
before my fairweather foes came,
those that crossed my fingers dumb.

Fault, fault, on both my houses –
Speed, bonny ark, and change your shape
until the ominous birds fly up.

# My Kingdom for a Horse

Having considered the place, having decided
There was not room enough, nevertheless
As nine o'clock shivered the dark balcony
I heard horses beating by;
And saw, below, white-coated riders, white-sided
Beasts blanketed against the cold and skyless
And groundless general benightment.
It was a white presentment
With one red light before, one red behind it.

'They pass every night.' Because
Of this I came to stay, small as it was.
Smaller still by daylight; much crockery
Had to go; many books were abandoned; so too,
A hoard of smooth planks, they had to go.

It is not altogether a mockery.
Horses alone I could not greatly care for,
But this by night is a company so corporate,
I call it a Horse, of regimental state.
Let no prodigal neighbour spend me therefore:
I am aware of this obvious school of riding,
And do not count it remarkable that late
And locally flies the Horse. What's to be wondered at
Is myself, that nightly to be dundered at
From a street without moment the whole length of it,
I mark the nine o'clock Horse, residing
Here, hemmed-in, on the strength of it.

# Intermittence

The old ridiculous partner is back again
who speaks my mind before me, singing me now
fonder than ever, my embarrassing vancourier.

I am her fool, the noisy one to follow
years at a time, and know her for my other
who sounds my superstition like a bagpipe.

I am her acrobat and altogether
lacking an answer loud enough I
somersault to her tune, how sick soever.

I left her once
for seven years long:
then she piped
and I did not dance.

Little it recks that
seven long years
I wept not
although she mourned,

since she is back again and the mood is on.

So must I bear my old she-wolf, who once
suckled the rising moon,
to blow her pipes, and I will dance again.

# Complaint in a Wash-out Season

My mind's in pickle. Think of my talents all soused
in rainwater, April you All Fool's Month, you've doused
the light of your joke. Call off this protracted
intransigent deluge, it's hackneyed;
nothing to grizzle about now – winter's gone knock-kneed,
so turn off the tap,
you monstrous infant wetting Infinity's lap.
You turned the garden hose on;
you spat a million missiles aslant through a hundred dozen
long-range peashooters. You should be past
practical jokes in bad taste;
and what an old has-been you look when you flash
in the face of the sun in a shot-silk taffeta sash
and lift the petticoat clouds and dance a fandango.
You've rinsed the guaranteed colours out of the rainbow.
At least, when you wash your dye-streaked hair,
be so kind as to shake it out elsewhere,
and request the adenoidal firmament
not to sneeze all over my temperament.

# Litany of Time Past

What's today?
>Hoops today.
What's yesterday?
>Tops yesterday.
What's tomorrow?
>Diabolo.

Moons and planets come out to play,
The Bear bowled, the Sun spun.
See the Devil-on-sticks run
Today, tomorrow, and yesterday.

What's Hope?
>Skipping rope.
What's Charity?
>Salty peppery.
What's Faith?
>Edinburgh, Leith,
>Portobello, Musselburgh,
>and Dalkeith.

Out you are.
>In you are.
Mustard.
>Vinegar.

# The Fall

The European Bison fell from grace.
So did the white-tailed Gnu.
Likewise the Blesbok, as also the Mountain Zebra.
The Giant Tortoise must have sinned too.

Everyone knows about the Dodo;
The same goes for the Great Auk.
The inoffensive Okapi's crime
Was trying to be other beasts at the same time.
And there is the case of the Blue-Buck.

They all came to a halt and are dissolved in mystery.
Who remembers, now, Steller's cullionly Sea-Cow?
It, too, through its innocent fault
Failed the finals in history.

TO18298

This one.

# Faith and Works

My friend is always doing Good
But doubts the Meaning of his labour,
While I by Faith am much imbued
And can't be bothered with my Neighbour.

These mortal heresies in us
Friendship makes orthodox and thus
We are the truest Saint alive
As near as two and two make five.

# Conundrum

As I was going to Handover Fists
I met a man with seven wrists.
The seven wrists had seven hands;
The seven hands bore seven bonds;
The seven bonds hid seven wounds:
How many were going to Handover Fists?

And as I was going to Kingdom Come
I met a dog of twenty ton.
The twenty ton had twenty parts;
The twenty parts bore twenty hearts;
The twenty hearts gave twenty barks:
How many were going to Kingdom Come?

# Note by the Wayside

To you, fretful exemplar, who claim to place
Love before all success and kindness above
Any career, I answer yes, well said, my dear,
If you have the particular choice:
If you're gifted, I mean, in love
And also special in life's performances.
But are you so very clever and so very nice?

# The Messengers

Arriving late sometimes and never
Quite expected, still they come,
Bringing a folded meaning home
Between the lines, inside the letter.

As a scarecrow in the harvest
Turns an innocent field to grief
These tattered hints are dumb and deaf,
But bring the matter to a crisis.

They are the messengers who run
Onstage to us who try to doubt them,
Fetching our fate to hand; without them
What would Sophocles have done?

# Fruitless Fable

Mr. Chiddicott, being a bachelor,
Purchased from a reputable department store
(Barkers') a morning-tea machine
At the price of fifteen pounds fifteen.
Easy to work, all plugged and wired.
Each night, he set the time required,
And every morning when he heard
The bell, he found his tea prepared.
But being by profession something mechanic
Mr. Chiddicott began to perfect it,
So that before long when it woke him up
It actually handed him the cup.

Years pass. Mr. Chiddicott grows
Successful as a cabbage rose,
Mellow, unmated and serene,
Served by the morning-tea machine.
Alas, the transience of bliss –
There came a sudden end to his.

One morning as it rang the bell,
The tea-machine said, 'What the hell,
I've stood this treatment long and dumb;
Mr. Chiddicott, the time has come
For you to make the tea instead.
Nip out and let me into bed.'
And when our friend demurred, alack,
The tea-machine gave him a dreadful crack.
Mr. Chiddicott murmured as he curled
Up, 'It is the end of the world.'

But it wasn't, for Mr. Chiddicott came
To, and finally admitted blame,
And every morning now he can be seen
(From the windows across the street, I mean)
Serving tea to his perfected tea-machine.

# Bluebell among the Sables

The visitor came clothed with sables,
My dark and social friend.
The afternoon prospered after its kind
But they bore me, those intimate parliaments,
Those tea-times wear my heart away.

So I took half my pleasure in the sables
That flowed across her arm, the chair, the floor,
Sleek and fathomless like contemplative,
Living animals, the deep elect,
In ceremonious most limp obedience.

But the dark skins did move, she felt them creep:
'My God! My sables!'
Indeed they were alive with a new life,
The sombre swiftly shot with quick and silver
Fur within fur. It was Bluebell, my beautiful,
My small and little cat pounding the sables.
Flat on her spine she tumbled them,
Shaking their kindly tails between her teeth.

'My furs! Your cat!' . . .
I said, 'No need for alarm;
Those dead pelts can't cause Bluebell any harm.'
(I am a human female and do not possess any sables.)
Poor soul, this put her in the wrong;
As one who somehow fails the higher vision,
She was meek: 'They cost the earth, my furs.'
I stroked the comical creature, she the sables,
And all came even.

For she said there was no damage, no damage.
It may be she had profit of the event;
As for myself that moment was well spent
When I saw Bluebell pummelling the sables.
I have the image, the gratuitous image
Miserly seized: of sable wonders glowing,
An order of the profound earth, of roots
And minerals evolved in civil strands,
Defined in which, the sprite, like air and like
A dawn asperges, green-eyed Bluebell plying
The sensuous fabric with her shining pads.

# A Visit

Sit in a chair.
Calm yourself in front of the fire
Because you have just arrived from a tour
Of No-Man's land.
No-Man took you by the hand.
No-Man showed you into a room
At the top of a tall emporium.
Nothing there
But a steel chair.
Nothing in it
But a filing cabinet.

And the steel chair said 'How do you do
I sent for you.
Meet my Cabinet
I was just going to reshuffle it.'
And he opened a drawer and reshuffled it.
Then said, 'Bring in
The dancing girl.' All shimmering
Came she dancing, breasts bare,
She had electric in her hair
Which gave you a shock.
Each breast was an alarm clock.
One was set at ten to two,
The other at a quarter past,
And you couldn't say which of them was slow
Or which of them was fast.
'Meet this lady,' said the steel chair.
'Notice her lever movements, dear.
You know she is a social improvement

Newly devised,
The first resistance movement
To be officially recognised.
Necessary to the race
At any time in any place;
Observe her charming contours ticking round
Because the hour is at hand.'

'Which is the hour?' you certainly said,
'On the left or on the right?'
'Ah,' said the girl, 'I can't decide,
But the alarm's not set tonight.'

'That's all for now,' said the steel chair,
'Show the gentleman out, my dear.'

# Industriad

There was some difficulty at first, hesitation
On the part of a nervous party who wanted to say
Something he couldn't recall; the Adult Education
Book had said it, that thing he wanted to say.

The managerial conference debate
Went on two hours like this until, slow
And tolerant, Piper got up to democrate,
With a university training behind him thirty years ago.

The face and form harmoniously convex.
He would, of course, say something statesmanlike,
Memorable. Piper was not sure
How to begin till a heavensent inspiration like
A splinter seemed to fly out of the floor:
'The human situation is becoming increasingly complex.'

In the car that night on the way to Sadler's Wells,
When he told his wife 'The human situation is
Becoming increasingly complex,' she thought her marriage
Well worth it, the way he put things in nutshells.

# *Communication*

Seeing them in that semi-exclusive place
One would have thought the couple perfectly suited;
She with a spherical, he with a conical face;
He a tubular outline; she, fluted.

So it came as a surprise to the listener-in,
And later, to recall, a diversion,
To find them versed in symbols, but alas, tuning-in
Each the wrong wavelength to a foreign station.

Take for instance his observation, 'I deplore
The present indiscriminate bankruptcy
Of flesh, time's daylight robbery.
I'm sure it has not been permitted before.'

Interrupted, however, by her statement, 'I
Shall try to get hold of seats for tomorrow and
See the robbers passing by:
A chance in a lifetime I understand.'

# *Verlaine Villanelle*

Like poor Verlaine, whom God defend,
I see the sky above the roof,
And write my book till summer's end.

When tree, town, bell and birdnote blend,
I feel, since summer sails aloof
Like poor Verlaine, whom God defend,

Who went to jail but did not mend.
I taste the pity sure enough
And write my book till summer's end.

I see a tree, and won't pretend
I'm warped on that nostalgic woof
Like poor Verlaine, whom God defend.

But rue the crooked dividend
These days will yield of galley-proof,
And write my book till summer's end.

Therefore I see the sky and spend
An hour of lyrical reproof,
Like poor Verlaine, whom God defend,
And write my book till summer's end.

# Edinburgh Villanelle

These eyes that saw the saturnine
Glance in my back, refused the null
Heart of Midlothian, never mine.

Hostile High Street gave the sign.
Holyrood made unmerciful
These eyes that saw the saturnine

Watchmen of murky Leith begin
To pump amiss the never-full
Heart of Midlothian, never mine.

Withal they left the North Sea brine
Seeping the slums and did not fool
These eyes that saw the saturnine

Waters no provident whim made wine
Fail to infuriate the dull
Heart of Midlothian, never mine.

Municipal monuments confine
What ghosts return to ridicule
These eyes that saw the saturnine
Heart of Midlothian, never mine.

# Holy Water Rondel

For salt, no word seems apposite;
Its common wisdom would defy
All praise, so far as meets the eye,
Salt is so meek a hypocrite.

And not the most selective wit
Has words to measure water by,
Because, so far as meets the eye,
Water is exquisite.

But cited sacerdotally,
Multiple evils up and quit,
Which proves that water and salt commit
Pathetic faults beyond the eye;

And shows a happy flaw whereby
The fabric is bereft of it,
Since there is nothing left of it
But mercies more than meet the eye.

Therefore I rate the creatures high
Whose salt and watery features knit
So strict and strange a composite
Of blessings and of brine thereby.

No wonder that the clergy ply
The people every week with it,
Who are of virtue infinite
So far as meets the eye.

# Shipton-under-Wychwood

Under Wychwood the growth and undergrowth
contend and do not mind how things exceptional
meander into landscape. They are drenched under
and under the repetitive green at last.
Fetched into chastity are fond extravagant
and noticeable doings and undertakings
whereover all the rhythms of Cotswold ride.

Ride, and have struck an ever-receding camp
over and over again, redundant time and tenses
disposing of themselves. What horses overtake them?
and what will become of the rare and royal hunters?
Prebend plunges over Plantagenet; it is all
over, then, with the legions of Rome before
finality, split-hooved, has taken over
Shipton under the forest, concealed in summer.

# Conversations

Two or three on the winter pavement talking,
One or two in the stubble field,
Idle, concerning miracles.

Voices are butter, but the eyes overtly
Detest another's dubious lips;
Eyes are blades where fancy breeds.

In boredom breeds, meanwhile remains to each
Enemy his friend, to every lying
Tongue an angel apiece.

The conversation therefore is in heaven,
Here on the streets of understanding
Here in the fields of bread.

When men are magic and air their advocates
Bide by the human grain and yet,
Though these offences needs must come,
Agree, sincere as light.

Blessed is the child of indiscretion talking,
And the orphan of indignation,
And before their Father's face, their conversations
Continually dancing.

Blessed are sons enticed to sea, and the mother
Constrained by wonder and by sign,
Their angels cover the face of the water,
And the water singeth a quiet tune.

Two or three must argue these contentions;
One or two in a winter season
Herein long since have plucked a sentiment or scandal.
But our conversation is in heaven.

# The Card Party

Pacified, smooth as milk, by cakes and tea,
Four ladies took their chairs accordingly;
Each, picking up her cards in slow suspense,
Preened up her creamy neck to Providence.

Somewhat apart from this important four,
Two sisters, knitting, settled near the door,
Cautioned each other, bending eye to eye,
Then watched the game together in rivalry.

Each player felt reluctantly compelled
To know what mystery the other held;
As one white neck rose taller with desire
The other three stretched likewise snakier.

And all the afternoon, discomfited,
Those four swans turned disdainful head from head;
Erect, they cast their cards throughout the night.
Each throat thinned upward like a stalagmite.

By dawn they bent and buried their flexible
Extending isthmuses beneath the table,
Upraising with apologetic pride
Those graceful members at the other side.

And what about the two beside the door?
They veered from cross to curious, hour by hour.
The knitting tangled, bound both necks askew,
And from this loggerhead a spiral grew

From which the sister-heads peered forth to pry –
What cards? All six got coiled there, finally.
Set in a formal knot and inextricable,
Two died beside the door, four at the table.

How brave these darlings, and how marvellous
That all their lovely necks should mingle thus.
Thus twined it was in death they coincided
Who always in their lives had been divided.

# Chrysalis

We found it on a bunch of grapes and put it
In cotton-wool, in a matchbox partly open,
In a room in London in winter-time, and in
A safe place, and then forgot it.

Early in the cold spring we said, 'See this!
Where on earth has the butterfly come from?'
It looked so unnatural whisking about the curtain:
Then we remembered the chrysalis.

There was the broken shell with what was once
The head askew; and what was once the worm
Was away out of the window, out of the warm,
Out of the scene of the small violence.

Not strange, that the pretty creature formalised
The virtue of its dark unconscious wait
For pincers of light to come and pick it out.
But it was a bad business, our being surprised.

# The Nativity

'Wind and slobber,' said the Flate, 'my words are
Slobber and wind whether I meet with another
Flate or no.   I say there is no other.
And I say what only another Flate can gather.
Either way, what I say is air and water.'


The Droom said, 'You're a sly one:
I was given to understand you were a Droom.
Look at your lips hewn out of sallow amber.
Look at your funny head all amethyst-encrusted,
Cut square. I should have known there is
No other Droom on earth. No one's to be trusted.'


'I', said the Aspontal, 'began to realise
We could hope only to be useful to each other
That time we three were looking at maps and
Plotting the journey together. We had to devise
Some reason for coming, and started saying "brother"
To each other. Don't brother me please in future,
You with the square head and you with the eyes
Inside your ears, for I never really
Believed you were Aspontals. However,
We've got to follow the star.
We've got to be three.
We've got to be wise.
Till heaven and earth pass
One jot or one tittle shall in no wise pass.'

## II. THE CONVERSATION OF THE SHEPHERDS

The Gladanka was saying, 'If a ewe gives
A dead lamb and you kick her three times thrice
In the face before sunset how many suns will
Rise before her blood stinks?' And the
Weezabaw laughed, rubbing his corns with a stone.
And the Shorket said, 'Sod the riddle the same as
You sodded the ewe.' The Gladanka was saying,
'I knew a ewe give a dead lamb every time
Till the farmer slit her belly and stuffed it back.'
And the Weezabaw laughed, 'Gladys,' he said,
'Gladys Barker was that ewe's name.' 'Sod the name,'
Said the Shorket, 'of the day I married the hollow-
Bellied Gladys Barker. If she's a Shorket
I'm a cherub with six eyes.' The Gladanka was
Saying, 'Your teeth grow out of your chin, you
No-Gladanka.' And the Weezabaw laughed;
'You two,' said the Weezabaw, 'you two will be
The death of me. You ought to see yourselves.
Whatever you both are is far, far
Short of a Weezabaw. You with the vertical mouth,
Keep in your tongue or it will wash your ears; and
You with the nose of top on your head, smell out
The principalities of heaven for all of us.'

## III. THE CONVERSATION AT THE INN

Samuel Cramer came down in the lift
And said, 'My bed's got bugs.
Where's the manager?'
And the girl at the desk replied, 'Not here.'

'Well find him quick,' said Samuel Cramer,
'My bed's got bugs.'
And the girl at the desk replied, 'What name please?'
'Samuel Cramer,' said Samuel Cramer.
'Not the poet!' said the girl at the desk.
'Well I used to be one,' said Samuel Cramer.
'How you've changed!' said the girl at the desk,
'you've done well for yourself, it's clear.'

'The manager, please,' said Samuel Cramer,
'I haven't a notion who you are.'
And the girl at the desk replied, 'He isn't here.
Don't you know La Fanfarlo the dancer?'

'You're the worse for the wear,' said Samuel Cramer,
'My bed's got bugs.'
And the Fanfarlo replied, 'I'll bump them flat for you
But no francs, please. We like dollars here.'

'Nothing doing,' said Samuel Cramer,
'Where's the manager?'
And the Fanfarlo replied, 'He's outside
Talking to a police inspector.'

'See, old soot,' said Samuel Cramer,
'I'm not here for your health.
I've come for a story for my paper.
What's going on round here?'

'The new tax,' said the Fanfarlo, 'We've got
A houseful of tax gatherers and tax payers;
And a man's wanted for murder, called Monteverde.
They think they've got him here. They say there's
Blood on his shirt and they were three days combing

The woods for him. A hot coming
*He* had of it I'm sure.'

'No good to me if it's local,'
Said Samuel Cramer.
'I thought there was going to be something big
According to a rumour.'

And the Fanfarlo replied, 'Clear out.'
'You anticipate me,' said Samuel Cramer.
'And pay before you go,' said the Fanfarlo.
'I'll see you in Hell,' said Samuel Cramer.

'I'll tell the manager,' yelled the Fanfarlo.
'Tell him,' said Samuel Cramer,
'That the bed's got bugs, the room reeks, and moreover
There's a mooing and bellowing going on
In the cattle shed beneath my window.
You'd think a cow was having a dozen
If it wasn't out of season.
But in this God-forsaken country anything could happen.'

IV. THE CONVERSATION OF THE ANGELS

Before the jubilees of Angels
    They said, 'What is that mess of meat and bone?'
Before the songs of Archangels
    They answered, 'That is no one.'

Before the concerts of Principalities
    They said, 'Who is no one?'
Before the dances of Virtues
    They answered, 'Man is no one.'

Before the lyres of Powers
   They said, 'Each man is one and Man is none.'

Before the voices of Dominations
   They said, 'Which man is like another one?'
Before the clamours of Thrones
   They answered, 'None is like another man.'

Before the thunders of Cherubim
   They said, 'To whom is each man known?'
Before the swift motion of Seraphim
   They answered, 'Each is known to no man.'

An Angel enquired of an Archangel, 'How many
Men have you seen?' And he replied, 'Plenty,
And women too. Divine affection
For them isn't easy. What a collection!'

A Virtue said to a Power, 'What ceases
When a man dies?' And he replied, 'A species,
Infinitely precious to God, being all
There is of his kind. He's irreplaceable.'

A Princedom asked of a Domination
'What is sin?' And he replied, 'The consumption
Of men by men. They've all got
An ache to eat what they are not.'

A Throne to a Cherub said,
'What do you reckon the price per head
Of men?' And he replied, 'I'm lost
Where sums are concerned. Ask the Holy Ghost.'

While the Seraphim got ready for the take-off –
    Six wings apiece, shot with bright shimmerings,
One said, 'What makes delight?'
    And one replied, 'The Queen of Heaven goes light.'
One said, 'What is to be made known?'
    And one replied, 'Men are to be made known.'
One said, 'What do these heavy six wings signify?'
    And one replied, 'Two to cover the face, two to cover the
        feet, and two to fly.'
One said, 'What do these dances signify?'
    And one replied, 'The resolution of discrepancy.'
One said, 'Fly, fly, for the love
    Of discrepancy most common.'
And one replied, 'Fly, fly,
    For the resolution of
    Common incongruity.'
One said, 'What's common to men?'
    And one replied, 'Uncommonness alone.
    Fly, for the grace
    Of common uncommonness
    Which is to be made known.
    Uncommon men become
    Common to men in Christ's face,
    Mediator of angels and of men.'

# Sisera

Sisera, dead by hammer and nail, fared worst
Where he fared well; the woman had fed him first.
After the kill Deborah came,
A holy kite to claim the heathen viscera.
Is not her song impressive? All the same,
I am for Sisera

Whose ruin had rhetoric enough and fitness
For Deborah's prophecy, so are God's enemies supplanted.
She needed no polemic, as God was her witness
Gloriously to publish the story condensed:
'The stars in their courses fought against
Sisera,' she descanted.

The hostess it was, who pinned the villain mute;
But Deborah whittled her fine art, the keener to spike him
On a final point: 'His women wait for the loot.'
So, from God's poets may God perfectly defend
Sisera and all the rest of us like him,
With whom the stars contend.

# *Canaan*

She is committed to earth, and the earth
Is plighted forever to her.
The wilderness is prone to her.
The hopeful race of all the earth is
Betrothed to her, pleasant ground of expectation,
Lambent country of Canaan.

Jordan heaved his banks away.
Jordan's valley bubbled over
High between those opposites.
He rose by night; he dipped by day.
He dipped down for the hosts of the wilderness
And for the silver country of Canaan.

The men of the wilderness at Jordan's ford
Lifted the Ark of the Covenant on their shoulders.
Jordan fled for all his worth.
Jordan-bed lay smitten to dry boulders.
The wilderness bore the Ark of the Lord
Of all the earth
Into the holy country of Canaan.

Canaan's the land where the wilderness landed.
Therefore I am not altogether confounded
Still to discover a wilderness in her.
Jordan shed his ways, lifted up the river;
Canaan's husbanded
Now with a ploughing sword, she is anointed
With burning torrents, bridal country,
Canaan of loss.

There goes that leviathan in his glory;
But here dissembles that wilderness. Fowl and beast
Have no more wonderful identity.
The tribes of the pomegranates and the tribes of the yeast,
The families of rubies and the families of grass
Are one to another as waste and waste
In the arms of Canaan of silver dross.


But I am not altogether confounded
That so immanent and green and promised a land
Confounds me with seeming not what she seemed;
Seeing the hopeful race is covenanted
Not less to Canaan
Than Canaan to her promised wilderness,
Seeing default of the double covenant, seeing
Treachery to the warm harvest, no gathering in
Of the pearly vines of Canaan.
The same thing over and over again.
In this I am not altogether bewildered.


No year is twice the same, nor has occurred
Before. We bandy by the name of grief,
Grief which is like no other. Not a leaf
Repeats itself, we only repeat the word.


    January, as usual, frigid. As before,
    A silent stir in February. More
    Of a stir in March. Activity
    In April, as previously.
    May, as usual, abundant. As before,
    A superfluity in June. Greenery galore
    Thereafter as always. The season exults.

But never the same season warily
Secretes the same petal from the same
Pod of a single bud. The circumstances are
Everywhere novel. The results
Only appear similar.

Time lacks experience. Therefore I am not quite
Confounded by history,
Being of the hopeful race of the earth,
Promised to promise, a mystery to mystery,
By which I am not altogether mystified,
Since she is plighted to me, a wilderness, and I to
The silver country of Canaan.

# FROM THE LATIN

Persicos odi, puer, apparatus:
Displicent nexae philyra coronae:
Mitte sectari, rosa quo locorum
    Sera moretur.
Simplici myrto nihil allabores
Sedulus curo: neque te ministrum
Dedecet myrtus, neque me sub arta
    Vite bibentem.

# Persicos Odi

(*Horace I, xxxviii,*
*in the Jacobean mode*)

Weave in my garland, boy, no more
The trash of Persia, and dispose
Therein not linden nor the rare
        Protracted rose.

Thus plainly twine the myrtle wreath
Which well accords thy servient mien,
And well thy master, drinking 'neath
        The trellised vine.

Solvitur acris hiems grata vice veris et Favoni:
    Trahuntque siccas machinae carinas.
Ac neque jam stabulis gaudet pecus, aut arator igni;
    Nec prata canis albicant pruinis.
Jam Cytherea choros ducit Venus, imminente Luna:
    Junctaeque Nymphis Gratiae decentes
Alterno terram quatiunt pede; dum gravis Cyclopum
    Volcanus ardens visit officinas.
Nunc decet aut viridi nitidum caput inpedire myrto,
    Aut flore, terrae quem ferunt solutae.

Nunc et in umbrosis Fauno decet immolare lucis,
    Seu poscat agna, sive malit haedo.
Pallida mors aequo pulsat pede pauperum tabernas,
    Regumque turris. O beate Sesti,
Vitae summa brevis spem nos vetat inchoare longam.
    Jam te premet nox, fabulaeque Manes,
Et domus exilis Plutonia: quo simul mearis,
    Nec regna vini sortiere talis;
Nec tenerum Lycidan mirabere, quo calet juventus
    Nunc omnis, et mox virgines tepebunt.

# To Lucius Sestius in the Spring

*(from Horace I, iv)*

A change in the weather. Winter's edge breaks to the soft west wind.
  Now they are rolling the dry keels down to the sea;
And the cattle no longer huddle in the stalls, nor the
      ploughman over his fire,
  Nor the fields blench frozen under a film of rime.

But Cythera (call her Venus if you like) is leading the dance now,
  By the light of the pendulous moon, her girls are linking
Delectable arms and shaking the earth with their feet,
      keeping time;
  Ferocious Vulcan's away meanwhile, inspecting his
      armaments factory.

Now's the time to dress yourself up: bind your brows with myrtle
  Or with your pick of the earth's yield; it's offered unstintingly;
Now is the time to sacrifice a lamb to the faun in the shadows
  Of the sacred wood – or give him a kid if he prefers it.

Know, Sestius, my lucky one, that pale impartial death will knock as hard
  At the gates of a royal fortress as he will at a small hut door.
Remember, there's only a lifetime to measure hope by,
  And night's got you marked already; old legendary
      ghosts move inward,

And not far below, there's a household of shades: once there,
      you'll never more
  Throw the dice for the odds of being wine-host,
Nor marvel at exquisite Lycidas who infatuates all the boys,
  Though the girls will soon begin to warm to him too.

Vides, ut alta stet nive candidum
Soracte, nec jam sustineant onus
Silvae laborantes, geluque
Flumina constiterint acuto.
Dissolve frigus, ligna super foco
Large reponens; atque benignius
Deprome quadrimum Sabina,
O Thaliarche, merum diota.
Permitte Divis caetera: qui simul
Stravere ventos aequore fervido
Deproeliantis, nec cupressi,
Nec veteres agitantur orni.
Quid sit futurum cras, fuge quaerere; et
Quem fors dierum cumque dabit, lucro
Appone: nec dulcis amores
Sperne puer, neque tu choreas.
Donec virenti canities abest
Morosa; nunc et campus, et areae,
Lenesque sub noctem susurri
Composita repetantur hora:
Nunc et latentis proditor intimo
Gratus puellae risus ab angulo,
Pignusque dereptum lacertis,
Aut digito male pertinaci.

# Winter Poem

(*from Horace I, ix*)

Look up at Mount Soracte's dazzling snow
Piling along the branches that can barely
   Withstand its weight, while piercing ice
     Impedes the river's flowing!

So, Thaliarch, let's dissolve the cold, stacking
The hearth with logs, and with a rash indulgence
   Fetch up the four-year vintage jars
     Of undiluted Sabine wine.

The rest leave to the gods at whose command
Contending winds and seething seas desist
   Until the sacred cypress-tree
     And ancient ash no longer quake.

Then cast aside this contemplation of
The future. Better reckon the random day's
   Advantage, child, and don't despise
     Parties and love and those sweet things.

While boyhood still forestalls cantankerous age,
Now is the time appropriate to whispered
   Seductive twilight messages
     In city courts and empty lots.

And now's your time for secret pleasantries
With a girl-friend mocking from her corner ambush –
   The time to steal a token from
     Her arm, or half-protesting finger.

Vivamus, mea Lesbia, atque amemus,
Rumoresque senum severiorum
Omnes unius aestimemus assis.
Soles occidere, et redire possunt:
Nobis, quum semel occidit brevis lux,
Nox est perpetua una dormienda.
Da mi basia mille, deinde centum,
Dein mille altera, dein secunda centum,
Deinde usque altera mille, deinde centum,
Dein quum millia multa secerimus,
Conturbabimus illa, ne sciamus,
Aut ne quis malus invidere possit,
Quum tantum sciat esse basiorum.

# Prologue and Epilogue
## (after Catullus)

PROLOGUE

*(Nox est perpetua una dormienda)*

Let's live Catullus, or else let us love –
One or the other, though rumour now
Lets live and love till the sun goes out.
The daylight lasts too long for us
Who follow after our wills' distortion
Along forevers of chosen darkness.

Those lovers were simple as fire but we
Advance into ice; they melted like rivers
But we are others; pale northman,
Resist that sun that shall offend you;
Be dumb, though time upon time I call
*Catulle* to the ancient stones or sing
These epithalamia always arrested.

Furi et Aureli, comites Catulli:
Sive in extremos penetrabit Indos,
Litus ut longe resonante Eoa
  Tunditur unda:
Sive in Hircanos, Arabasque molles,
Seu Sacas, sagittiferosque Parthos,
Sive qua septemgeminus colorat
  Aequora Nilus:
Sive trans altas gradietur Alpes,
Caesaris visens monumenta magni
Gallicum Rhenum, horribilesque, ulti-
  mosque Britannos:
Omnia haec, quaecunque feret voluntas
Caelitum, tentare simul parati,
Pauca nuntiate meae puellae
  Non bona dicta;
Cum suis vivat, valeatque moechis,
Quos simul complexa tenet trecentos,
Nullum amans vere, sed idemtidem omnium
  Ilia rumpens.
Nec meum respectet, ut ante, amorem;
Qui illius culpa cecidit, velut prati
Ultimi flos, praetereunte postquam
  Tactus aratro est.

# EPILOGUE

*(Furi et Aureli, comites Catulli)*

You, Hate and Love, companions of this poet
Where cities of fire sustain me, and where
The glaciers clash together the northern tundras'
      Assaulted waters,

Shall face these weathers of my instruction.
Then travel courageously, notorious couriers
Into the icelock, and beyond its zero
      Seek out my love.

Remind him first of all how he survives
The flower of death blown over that relinquished
Meadow where lover and plough break
      Lover and flower alike.

But let him not believe that a winter invoked
Can blight the bespoken summers nor silence him
Being that one who called time upon time,
      *Lesbia* to the ancient stones.

Stockton - Billingham
LIBRARY
Technical College